MW01127474

Voices From My Heart

A Collection of Poetry

By Vanassa Branch

iUniverse, Inc.
New York   Bloomington

Voices From My Heart

A Collection of Poetry

This is a work of fiction. All of the characters, names, incidents, organizations, and dialogue in this novel are either the products of the author's imagination or are used fictitiously.
iUniverse books may be ordered through booksellers or by contacting:

iUniverse
1663 Liberty Drive
Bloomington, IN 47403
www.iuniverse.com
1-800-Authors (1-800-288-4677)

ISBN: 978-1-4401-3016-8 (pbk)
ISBN: 978-1-4401-3017-5 (ebk)

Printed in the United States of America

iUniverse rev. date: 03/20/2009

This Collection of Poetry

is dedicated

To the memory of my mother and father

Ezell Jimmerson-Macon

February 25, 1927 - June 23, 2008

Walter Ridley Anderson

June 13, 1937 - September 23, 1958

Contents

Introduction

One day I heard a co-worker state, she's got the right look we need for the job. I thought how often the right look can be deceiving. The well dressed lady walks pass us with her head held high, shoulders back, each step graceful and confident left us in awe over that look. But she moved so swiftly, we missed the sadness in her eyes. Moving swiftly is how many of us cope with our day to day trials. If we slowed down long enough, someone may see our vulnerability making us targets. At age 12, I wrote my first poem, "I Never Knew My Father". It was my way of coping and rationalizing the sadness that sometimes ate at my soul. From that day forward, pen and paper accepted my vulnerability without criticism or pity. My father's family never made any efforts to know me, nor I them.

A few years ago, I began sharing my poems with two close co-workers, Lisa and Gertie. They gave me the inspiration and courage to work toward publishing my own collection of poetry. Through this process, I have grown in faith, maturity and found peace. Without fear of what others may think, I embrace my passions (singing in the church choir and writing poetry.) My church family has been very supportive of my efforts and I sincerely appreciate that.

Poems in this book represent different phases of my life and the various emotions and people shaping those experiences. Chapter 1 is dedicated to momma and families losing love ones to dementia.

She was and continues to be my inspiration. My mother was also my friend and shopping buddy. She died June 23, 2008, four years after being diagnosed with dementia. "Over There" was written November 17, 2004 the day we were informed of her diagnosis. During a family meeting, her doctor, social worker, and psychologist informed the family that over time, her mental and physical functions would decline. Over time Momma forgot how to walk, sit up, and feed herself. Her thoughts became jumbled. She struggled with words. It was difficult for her to put complete sentences together. But, she praised God even on her death bed. I asked her one day, what are you going to do when you go to heaven? I could see her struggling for words until, see God, came gushing out and we both giggled with delight. During her decline in functions, "Shuffling Along", "I Can", and "Have You Seen My Momma" were a few poems written. "A Broken Heart", "I Got My Wings", "Collection of Tears", "Journey", and "Missing You" were written after her death.

I would like for you to take this journey with me through my collection of poetry. Pray, cry, laugh, love, but most of all find peace and embrace simplicity. I did.

Chapter 1 - Dedication to Momma

Portrait of Love

Smothering stares from the sun
compels beads of moisture
to trickle down her soul

Cotton sack draped across her shoulder
Fit perfectly, a tailored made glove
Its weight pressed deeply
into her flesh

Fighting temptation to glance at rows
of emptiness left behind
Embarking upon rows ahead
three mouths to feed
another on the way

As a child
Yelled at, belittled, spit on
By strangers passing by
Harboring supremacy

My mother, a silhouette
Of Africa American beauty and pride
Unshaken, unmoved, pressed
On her five mile pursuit
For intellectual bliss
And equality

Like her ancestors who were stolen onto
Filthy crowded ships
Held in captivity
Hard work, hardship, heartache
Were her intimate acquaintances

Rows of white stretched as
Far as the eyes could see
Driven by the little brown face with auburn eyes
Gazing up from where she lay, on the cotton sack
Conquering one row at a time

When night fell, she whispers a prayer
As the moon cast shadows upon their angelic faces
sleep well my babies, hunger takes no hostages tonight

A Mother's Touch

When I was born
You claimed me
When the doctor announced a girl
You named me

Fed and clothed me
When I'd cry
You'd hold me

When I was troubled
You saw it
Gave me strength
Through all of it

Thank you mother
For that gentle touch
Thank you mother
For loving me that much

A Mother So Dear

A hush covered me like a blanket
As I lay in the comfort of my bed
I prayed thanking God
For his blessings, especially
For a mother so dear

Thoughts drifted to the day
I gazed upon her
With such intensity
Sketching her deep inside

Pride rose within my heart
Eyes dampen with tears
She never knew the fear
Welling within

Before me stood a lady
Strong, smart, full of wisdom
Eager to help her neighbor
God's humble servant

A true mother not only
To her children
To anyone willing to give her
A moment of their time

My advisor, my friend
My mother
A gift from God
A mother so dear

Over There

Leaves are changing colors
Falling from the trees
Right before my eyes
You're drifting away from me

Where are your going?
But got this long and peaceful stare
With a smile, you replied
I'll just be over there

We have more shopping to do
More talks to have
More laughter too
There're lots more things
For us to do

With this long peaceful stare
And a smile, you replied
I'll just be over there

So many times you have put
My troubled heart at ease
If you should go too far
And I can't see your face
Hear your voice
Know that you're near
I will lose my way
I will not stay

My dear child, you replied
You'll not lose your way
And you will stay
Because, I raised you that way

If you should need me
And when you do
You'll see my face
Hear my voice
Know that I'm near
Because I'll just be over here

Shuffling Along

We stood in the middle of the floor
Shuffle here
Shuffle there
We were going no where

Pain went cascading through my heart
Tears rolled down each cheek
Old man time
Wouldn't let momma move her feet

Don't let him win
I wanted to shout
Then momma started
Moving slowly about

Where did she go
That vibrant woman I used to know
As the lump in my throat
Continued to grow

For her sakes
I put my emotions intact
Because my voice
Had started to crack

I gained my composure
To escape my exposure
And my momma went
Shuffling along

I Can

I can only imagine
What it would feel like
To live in a reality
All of your own

I can see and hear
Your frustrations your struggles
To hold on
One more day

I can love you
For who you were
Yesterday, today, tomorrow
And thereafter

It's your strength
Your faith, love for your family
That I can feel
Deep down inside
Deep down inside

Have You Seen My Momma

Have you seen my momma
That's her in bed
That's not my momma
That lady doesn't talk
That lady doesn't walk

My momma loves to talk
And for us unlimited miles
She'd walk!

And she wouldn't be in bed
Momma would be in the kitchen
Cooking mustard greens
Making corn bread

I'm warning you
Mr. Dementia or whoever
You claim you are
Where's my momma

He led her to the bedside
She stood there and cried
Momma!
It is you

I Got My Wings

It was never my intention
To break your hearts
To make you cry
Grown old, tired, and die

God sent his angel
She gently stroked my cheek
Sang such a sweet melody
I guess I fell asleep

When realizing what had happened
I was suspended mid-air
You were gazing upon my body
Still laying there

Your weeping and your wailing
Crushed my aching heart
God's angel waited patiently
Until I was ready to depart

Calling you name by name
I blew a farewell kiss
Thought of our lives together
And how you would be missed

I whispered into the oldest ear
Asked her to tell the rest
To fulfill their dreams
Always give God their best

I turned to face God's angel
Embraced her comforting smile
Eyes pleaded your weeping
Would last for just awhile

She covered me with heavenly wings
When released I had wings too
She gazed into blue gray skies
I knew what I had to do

As I started on my journey
Lighting illuminated the sky
Revealing my page within the book
Held by the King on high

I soared into majestic skies
I could hear your weeping still
But today, I got my wings
And that was God's will

A Broken Heart

Silver skies opens and delivers
Her thunderous cries
Into bosoms of heaven

Intensive urge to release explosive
Fervent fiery, invades
Her deepest darkest depths

Legs like noodles, give way
To the heaviness within, paralyzing
Every inch of her brokenness

Shivering from intrusive reflection
Of cold flesh, longing warmth
And security of her mother's womb

Cradling her brokenness
Restraining her brokenness
Unleashing her brokenness

Journey

If our weeping should
Deluge the land
There would be no solid ground
To firmly plant our feet

We would plummet
Into dens of moles
Worms would squish
Between our toes

Or, we could
Swing upon oceans
Of clouds
Sing paradisal ballads aloud

Upon a sparrow's wing
We would be weightless
In flight
And soar toward stars of light

Missing You

Children playing
Laughter ringing
Sadness and loneliness
Churns within the belly
Of self-pity

My heart carries the load
From my shoulders
Anger and grief
Held hostage
Within my soul

Hour glass of life
Reflects a motherless,
Fatherless child

Times like these
I yearn comfort
Of your voice
Your presence
Your unconditional love

Collection of Tears

Silent air suffocates
Palpitations within, crack
The foundation of what was
And grief swells
Like rivers rising against dams

I'm drowning
In a river of red tears
Collecting at the base
Of momma's heart

Birthed from roots
Deep and strong
Her peaceful glow
Embraces restful bliss

Her woven tapestry
Of charisma and courage
Forever engraved
Rescues me
From my drowning heart

I Never Knew My Father

I never knew my father
He died sometime ago.
He died before I was born
A girl he'd never know.

Some say I resemble him
In certain little ways.
I have the ability to be happy
On any kind of days.

What does it feel like
To call someone dad?
I'm sure it's a great feeling
A feeling I never had.

I asked my mother
What was my father like?
She said he was a kind man
A man people liked.

I wish I had known him
Like others know their dad.
But I guess it wasn't meant for me
Because my life might have been sad.

Chapter 2 - Peace

Victory

She looked at defeat
In her darkest hour
Gave it to her father
With all the power

She heard a soft voice
Go to sleep my child
For victory is your
In just a little while

When she rose
At the break of day
In her heart she knew
Everything would be ok

She looked toward Heaven
Beyond the sky, so blue
She saw love, peace, joy
And sweet victory too

I Can Fly

One night I dreamed I could fly
Soaring across the sky
Gazing upon this world
From on high
So filled with joy
I started to cry

I spread my arms
As if they were wings
I stoked the air
So gracefully it seemed

As I rested my arms
Down by my side
I started to glide
And enjoy the ride

I wondered what did this mean
As I looked down at this wondrous scene
Was I caught in between
Was I human or heavenly being

Suddenly I was awaken
By a familiar sound
Without hesitation
My feet hit the ground

Still in the flesh nevertheless
No longer had feelings
Of hopelessness

The Long Journey Home

When I started on this journey today
There was a warm embrace upon my face
I gazed to the North, South, East and West
I observed no one in distress

My thoughts went to the long journey home
Thinking I was all alone
I saw the trees swaying side to side
My first instinct was to run and hide

I planted my feet as I stood there
Even though I was in despair
I closed my eyes, gritted my teeth
I felt a push and shove but did not bulge

Something wet fell upon my cheeks
The clouds had sprung a leak
I saw flash of lightning heard a loud clapping roar
As I caught a glimpse of my front door

Something beautiful appeared across the sky
A rainbow of colors caught my eye
I stopped dead in my tracks
Admiring it never looking back

Sweet smelling fragrance filled the air
Flowers blooming everywhere
The grass was as green as green could be
I had never discerned such beauty around me

The door opened without use of my key
What I found inside was peace
I was never alone it was God's love
That brought me on this long journey home

Surrender

Affectionately embracing simplicity
Basking in sacrificial love

Intoxicating sights and sounds
And laden scents

Surrendering to simplicity
Surrendering to serenity

Solitude

Sitting at the kitchen table
Sipping my morning brew
A new day filters through droplets
Nesting against my window pane

Energized
With a surge of newness
Thoughts blank like an artist canvas
Awaiting creation of a masterpiece

Embracing moments of solitude
I will bottle its seductive affect
And splash beauty upon the canvas
Of my renewed soul

Simple and Free

Imminent submission
Of my being, essence of my soul
New chapters of existence
Begin to unfold

Bolts and nuts
Of shackles binding me
Departed stubbornly
Setting me free

Free from clutter hidden
Behind wood stained doors
Free from self induced chaos
Parading life's overloads

Free from decomposed fears
Decaying within my flesh
Free from afflictions
Robbing me of rest

Simple and free within richness
Of love, life, and laughter
Simple and free
Stamped within pages
Of fruitful chapters

Chapter 3 - Humor

The Dog's Bowl

How much sweeter could it get
Watching a child and his pet
In the yard playing fetch

I walked away for just a minute
To return and find both heads in it
The dog's bowl

Both eating like there was no tomorrow
While I stood there in horror
Get out of there I managed to holler

I called my mother
She said he would be ok
But the image in my head said no way

My little boy ate from
The dog's bowl

Use Scope

Why did you brush my toothbrush
Over the soap
All you had to say was
Mom use scope

Did you think I needed
To wash my mouth clean
All because I said
A few ugly things

I love you
My little mischievous child
But what you did
Was foul

Rubbing your momma's toothbrush
Over the soap
Next time tell me
To use scope

A Reflection Of Me

I went to this restaurant
To have myself some lunch

I decided to eat from the buffet
I was really hungry that day

I walked from island to island
Boy was I smiling

I got a little of this, little of that
Person beside me must thought we'd met

All up in my personal space
I wanted her out of my face

With hands on my hip, head spinning around
If I got lip girlfriend's going down

I turned around to give her this look
But became so amused my body shook

A reflection of me is what I saw
In the mirror next to the slaw

Daddy Told Me Last Night

I sat in the corner all day long
I didn't care anyway
My daddy told me last night
Hitting his big boy wasn't right
And if they hit me
Hit'em back

I'm only three going on four
I will not be bullied anymore
I walked into that daycare ready for battle
Knowing that the teachers couldn't paddle

Maybe they hit me
Last week or yesterday
Today they all had to pay
When I started swinging I didn't quit
Until all those bullies had been hit

Thanks dad for that bit of advice
Now they're treating me nice
We're running around having fun
No one's hitting me with their toy gun

Stuff Happens

An amusing occurrence
Transpired the other day
A man purchased a burger
And went on his way

When ready to relax and eat
Discovered he had no meat

I bet his head started to spin
Jumped in his car
And then…

I observed him
Galloping our way
Upon examining his purchase
I had nothing to say

The man had no meat!

Chapter 4 - Rhymes

Momma's Joy

Just as I decided to give up
There was nothing left
I wanted to do
God blessed me with you

I would sit and stare
At your little face
And thank him
For his mercy and grace

He knew he had to
Save me from me
I was sinking deeper
And deeper into a selfish sea

He knew
I wanted a little boy
He gave me you
You gave me joy

You're perfect, to me
In every little way
Even though, you don't
Always do what I say
Or do it my way

You're the love of my life
My sweet little boy
You're momma's happiness
You're momma's joy

Unconditional Love

Through rain, sleet, and snow
Your tears spill ashore

Through warm summer breeze
Saintly shadows of trees

Through fields of cattles, grazing
His love is amazing

Through your suffering and pain
Call upon his holy name

He sees your broken parts
His love will mend your broken heart

The Campers

What a cute couple they make
Our pastor and his gorgeous mate
They came to us six years ago
And we've watch their family grow

The first lady has a contagious smile
That can be seen for miles
And that little man, we call our preacher
He's a dynamic speaker

He tells us what God wants us to know
And encourages us to grow
When they came to us
They had two young girls
Then, came along a rambunctious little boy with curls

He's as cute as he can be
We all know who's in charge of that family's tree
(Sorry Pastor, but it ain't thee)

Camper family our meeting
Was not by accident
He waited for your response (I will go)
Then you were sent

Where Will He Sleep Tonight

In route to work
I drove passed this proud man
Unlike the Good Samaritan
Didn't lend a helping hand

He was slender built
Of average height
I wondered
Where he would sleep tonight

Oversized hat
Upon his head
His pillow wherever
He made his bed

Shopping cart
Filled with stuff
All he owned, confirmation
Life's been rough

From my rear view mirror
I sneaked another peek
Compassion anoints
My soul's meek

Forfeit opportunity
To extend a helping hand
Adhering to the Master's
Divine command

Gazing back
Until I lost his sight
Still, inquisitive
Where he would sleep tonight

Restless Souls

Who walked away with the prize
Or was it just about getting a thrill
From telling those lies
Destroying others lives

Two adults, consenting
To deceive, To destroy
To deliver hurt and pain
To those sharing their names

I feel sorry for their restless souls
One day they shall grow old
Then who will they hold
When those they hurt, hearts are cold

Buck

Early one Sunday morning
The phone rang
Buck's gone, the caller said
Right away she knew that meant
He was dead

She questioned the caller
On the phone
What do you mean
Buck's gone

He had no time
To say goodbye
Received his wings
And orders to fly

She cried out
As she tossed the phone
Fell to her knees
Screamed, my brother is gone

When the day came
She watched his lifeless body
Once filled with zest
Laid beneath the soil
So that, his soul could rest

A few days later
He appeared to her
As a child in a dream
And she thought, what did this mean

He was in an open field
Running and jumping
In the grass so high
Perhaps, he was telling her goodbye

He smiled in his playful
And mischievous way
Then went running and jumping
Farther away

She saw
He was having fun
As he disappeared
Into the sun

She tried to reach him
Without success
But found comfort
In seeing his playfulness

To My Nephew

Hey little nephew
Why your heart so sad
You trusted the devil
Now you done gone
Made him mad

Got yourself locked up
Guess you're wondering
What da....

Is that the place
You want to be
Behind bars
Daylight, you don't see

Another of his soldiers
Off the street
Soul snatching thief
Don't tolerate defeat

He's been plotting
Since you've been away
In anticipation
Of your exit day

He'll be waiting
To befriend
Reel you back
Into a life of sin

He wants you weak
Feeling alone
He wants your soul
Nephew be strong

Tell that devil
To get under your feet
Tell that devil
You're done with his deceit

Self-Righteous

They passed us by
Never acknowledging we're there
Gawking straight ahead
With their self-righteous stare
Beckoning us to get in their way
 If we dare

Self-righteous dressed
In their glorious attire
With an inner appearance
Only they can admire
Having self-righteous justice
Only they can conspire

They live in a world
Of make believe
Thinking everything they get
They should receive
No matter how it was achieved

These Matters

Beware
Of smiling faces
Hidden behind
Fake embraces

With hidden agendas
They lay and wait
To capitalize on
Your mistakes

Small minds
With eyes on the gold
Lacking the faith
That would make them whole

If you must, shed a tear
Say a pray or two
God sees and hears
All that they do

He promises
To fight your battles
So, be still
And place in his hands
These matters

Children of Today

Children of baggy pants
Seductive dance
Proud walks
Suggestive talks

Should we lock'em up
Throw away the key
Should we let'em run free

We can't let'em go astray
Our ancestors paved the way
So we'd have a say
And to instill hope
Into our children of today

My Feeling Has Been Hurt

Crying until my eyes hurt
Eyes are blood shot red
I have this hurting feeling
I wish that I was dead

Everything is closing in
I want room to shout
My eyes can't take no more
This feeling it must come out

I never felt this way before
This feeling I can't explain
It's really getting next to me
It's driving me insane

A Working Mother

A Working Mother
Never misses a beat
Even when
She's dead on her feet

To help support her family
She works everyday
That never gets
acknowledged anyway

After work, she run errands
Pay a few bills
Despite her aching feet
From wearing high heels

When she's about
To head for the house
She gets a call on the cell
From her spouse

When given another task
To do
Remembers
She has to gas up too

One foot in the back door
Bags in her hands
Momma what are you cooking
Came from the other end

Putting her purse and bags
On the kitchen table
Wonders if today
She will be able

She was true
To her calling
A working mother
Never missing a beat
Even when
She was dead on the feet

It Ain't About You

I guess you thought
because the sun was shining
this morning
No rain clouds in the sky
You were the reason why

I guess you thought
because you minded your
own business
Stayed in your own little world
Never asking for nothing
expecting even less
You'd never have to deal with any mess

I guess you thought
because your so called friends
walked away
You didn't need them anyway

I guess you thought
because you go to church
on Sundays
sit there all proud and proper
On those pews
Paying your self-determined dues
That was all expected of you

It Ain't About You

I guess you thought
because you worked hard
paid your bills on time
They ought to get theirs
where I got mines

Too afraid to step out of
your comfort zone
Too much pride to admit
when you're wrong

It Ain't About You

I'm pleading with you
To open up your heart
 allow God to fill every part
With unconditional love
For your brothers, your sisters
Those madams, those misters
Now can you hear silent whispers

It Ain't About You

When You Believe

When you believe
There's no room for self pity
Besides the sight of it
Is never pretty

When you believe
There's no room for self-doubt
You'll never take
The coward's way out

When you believe
Sky's the limit
And you can have
All that's in it

You'll stand up and fight
For your constitutional rights

A Woman's Prayer

Oh heavenly father, for just one day
Make me a star in the sky
That gives light; that shows the way
For someone who had no hope that day

With a big smile and a watchful eye
I'd give the light, I'd show the way
And pray for blessings, that day

Oh heavenly father, I pray
To be a star in the sky
No extra brightness, no stand out glare
Just among those that care

I'd give the light
I'd show the way
I'd pray for blessings
For someone with no hope that day

Chapter 5 - Non-Rhymes

I'm Grief

The reality of it
Is that it doesn't really
Feel like reality at all

Going through the motions
Why?
What's the purpose?

Walking outside the body
Looking in
Longing to touch the hurt
Massage it
Make the pain go away

This too
They say, shall pass
If I should say, NO
What then?

Can't you feel my pain
How dare you forget my name
Carrying on
As if nothing has changed

You, world
Stops for nothing or no one, I see
Not even me
No matter how brief
Who am I?
I'm grief

The Battle Within

Bulging glares of river red
Invoke temperamental waves
Breaking rocks
Into boulders, pebbles, and sand

Demonic forces battle
Within crevices
Of disappointments, pain,
Fear

Graciously, she bows and retreats
Unto turbulent warfare
Submissive and obedient, tribulations
Cast into dungeons of hell

The Pleas

Fate slipping
Into cracks of crusted living
And you're sporting
Harvest in mid-July

Kaleidoscope of innocence
Filtering black clouds
Your destiny in the hands
Of a gavel and a black robe

Plead
Remorse
Regret
Rehabilitated

Day Gone Bad

Overhead sun rays shimmer
I lift my face to absorb its warmth
As a flock of geese ascend
In V formation
One two three four .....
My count interrupted
An unpleasant wet substance
Descends
Showering my
Dry cleaned white blouse

I Ponder

As I drove pass the scene
Of an accident where someone
I knew met death,
My mind began to wonder
I thought of her and my brother
And began to ponder over death.

Does it mean a body
Without a soul?
A soul without a body?
When it's all around you,
Can you see it, taste it,
Smell it, or hear it?

How does its presence
Make a strong man cry?
A weak woman strong?
Be a heartbreaker and comforter
All at the same time?

I don't ever expect to know
The answers to such questions
I do expect that I will ponder
Over these questions again someday

Endless Possibilities

The sting of my past
Has departed
My future steps
Ordered with endless possibilities

Bold and fearless
Each possibility
A milestone
A stepping stone

Walls tumbling down
Doors opening
Visions of I can,
It can be, it can happen

Circling like vultures
Being seized
And conquered
By their rightful owner

No time to celebrate
Celebrating clouds the visions
And interrupts the flow
Of endless possibilities

Poverty

The hairs on the back of my neck
Stood erect from the breeze
Of his sweltering tainted breath

His long contorted fingers
Slithered over my shoulder
Sending shock waves of disgust

He proclaims long time acquaintance
Of the family; calls my name
His bass distorts its natural poetic flow

Summoning my baby browns
To confront destitution
With a humble awakening

The "I" Syndrome

Foolish boasting like venom spews
From the mouth of self-righteousness
Empty words collapse upon muted ears

Foolishness enters the heart
And corrupts the soul
Favor does not lie
Within depth of foolish boasting

Such things prophesized
Giving wisdom and
Infinite insight
Into God's magnificent grace

Where Will The Heart Be Found

When sadness has turned
Into anger
When anger has turned
Into hate
And hate has taken
Your soul
Where will the heart
Be found?

Fight or Flight

Intense heat
Trapped beneath the surface
Seeking means of escape
Pressures of the world
Lying dormant deep within
Crevices of your soul
Fight or flight?

What Am I

I'm a twinkling light
A breath of fresh air
I'm as light as a feather
I glow in the dark
What Am I?

I'm a warm embrace
With electrifying energy
I'm as wide as an ocean
As deep as the sea
I can be salvation
What Am I?

Awaken

Awaken by wailing sirens
and tires pounding pavement

Reverberation ringing
long after its passing

Motionless energy creeps
Into murky corners of wonder

Gradual migration toward the
Comatose stage in which I came

There Are Those

There are those
Articulating elegant words
That flow fluently
Like never ending rivers

Comfort of them
Soothing to the ear
Temporarily easing the ache
Concealed within your heart

There are those
Who stumbles and stutters
Over words, by your side
They journey with you
To that place
Of purgatory and back again

Flight of Eagles

Feeble cries
Shuffle of feet
Echoing
Throughout phantom halls

Roaming starving eyes
Velvety skin,
Wrinkles of time
Unveiling life stories

Graciously embracing
Woes of yesteryears
Man made tear drops
Prolong inevitable journey

Ascending,
Transcending
Free spirits
Mocking time

Close

Close
The distance
Goes for miles and miles

Our youthfulness stolen
Not by old man time
You stole from me
I stole from you

Our long and mysterious journey
Of two forgotten identities
Struggling one
Against the other

Perhaps, this journey
Was not what we expected
Or even hoped for
But it is, what it is

The path not traveled
Resembles the path already traveled
And the distance
Goes for miles and miles

A Man Is A Man

Perspiration escapes
His brow producing a
Brackish trail of perseverance

A flaming star
Will rise and set
Upon his leathery flesh
Before exhaustion prevails

My nephew
Carved of dignity and integrity
Connect dots
Of scattered dreams

Flirting with persistent
Discomfort, acknowledges
Blessed be the day
A man is a man

Dreams

Listen to your heart
Pumping dreams
Through veins of hope
For brighter days ahead

Unwanted unhealthy emotions
Toxin to the beauty
Within the grace
Of your soul

Give dreams eyes to witness
Legs to climb monstrous hills
Arms to stretch toward
Majestic skies

The Clock

With the ball in hand
I gaze upon my playground
My day to shine
All eyes on me
The clock ticks silently
With grace and lightning speed
I seize the moment
Ten, nine, eight, seven
Weaving left and right
A breeze settles upon
My opponent's cheek
As I brush by
Six, five, four
The ball leaves my hand
Three, two
No worries
I'm free

Nubian Goddess

Gaze upon me, I'm beautiful
Not because of my skin color
Texture of my hair
Complexity of my being
Accept me!

My eyes may be brown
My nose a little wide
My lips a little full
My hips…

Infinitely praised
Embrace me!

God made me
Molded me
Into this perfect creation
Gave me
Mind, Body, and Soul

When you gaze upon me
Don't tell me what you see
I already know

I'M A BEAUTIFUL BLACK WOMAN!